W9-BOB-740

The Dino Pals Picture Dictionary

Illustrated by Jan Lewis

BACKPACKBOOKS
NEW YORK

a b c d e f g h i j k l m n o p q r s t u v w x y z

Aa

above

Dippi's head is above the trees.

add

If you add two apples to three bananas, you have five pieces of fruit.

address

This is the address where the Dino Pals live.

afraid

Are you afraid of these big dinosaurs?

airport

The airplane is taking off from the airport.

alone

Red is sad. He is all alone and there is no one to play with him.

alphabet

The dinosaurs are learning the alphabet from A to Z.

always

Little Dinosaur always wears a red scarf with white dots.

animal

Dinosaurs are animals. Lots of animals live on the farm as well. Some animals can fly, some can swim, and some can do both. You are an animal, too!

answer

1 + 1 = ?

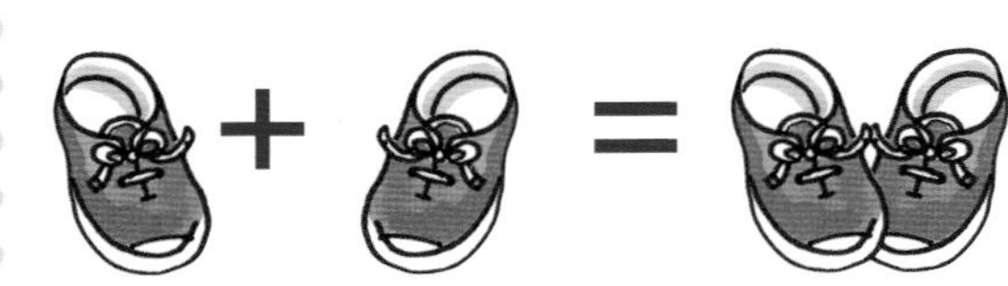

The answer is 2.
Did you get the answer right?

ant

An ant is a little insect. You often see lots of ants together.

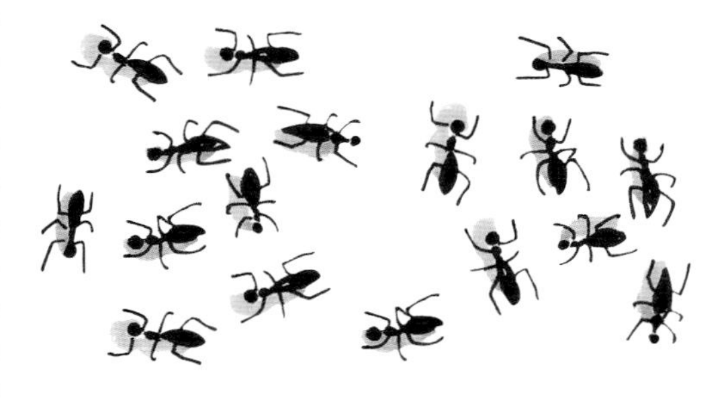

apple

When you eat an apple, only the core is left. Apples grow on trees. They are fruit.

arm

This is Little Dinosaur's arm. How many arms do you have?

artist

Red enjoys painting. He wants to be an artist when he grows up!

asleep

Red is asleep.

astronaut

An astronaut travels into space in a rocket.

awake

Dippi is awake. He is reading a book. His friends are all asleep.

Bb
baby
Baby Dinosaur is very young.
She cannot walk yet.
back
This dinosaur has
spikes on her back.
bag
Little Dinosaur is carrying a
pink bag. He is going shopping.
ball
This looks like an
exciting game!
Can you see the
red ball?
banana
Remember to peel
the banana
before you
eat it!
bathtub
Dinosaurs need a
really big bathtub.
beach
Red is running
on the beach.
Dippi is wading
in the water.
bear
Little Dinosaur loves his toy
bear. He calls it Teddy.
a b c d e f g h i j k l m n o p q r s t u v w x y z

a b c d e f g h i j k l m n o p q r s t u v w x y z

box

This box is full of toys.

boy

This boy is called Benjamin. His name begins with B.

bread

The Dino Pals like sandwiches, so they buy lots of bread.

bridge

The Dino Pals go over this bridge on the way to school.

building

The dinosaurs have been to the city to see the buildings. Now they are waiting for the bus home.

bus

busy

Tricky is busy. He is painting a picture.

butterfly

Little Dinosaur is watching the butterfly.

buy

Dippi is shopping. He needs to buy some apples.

a b c d e f g h i j k l m n o p q r s t u v w x y z

Cc

cake

The cake has pink frosting.

card

Look at the cute picture of a cat on this greeting card.

carry

Carry that big cup of coffee very carefully, Little Dinosaur!

castle

This castle has high walls. It is not easy to get inside.

cat

The Dino Pals' pet cat is called Lucky. He is a black and white cat.

catch

Red is trying to catch the orange balloon. Be careful not to burst it!

chair

The chair is blue. It has a red cushion on the seat.

cheese

Dippi loves to eat cheese.

chicken

How many chicks does this chicken have?

children

These children are playing with their pets.

clean

Dippi is having a bath and scrubbing his neck. It's clean now.

climb

Little Dinosaur is trying to climb to the top of the tree.

clock

Can you see the time on the clock? It is time for the dinosaurs to come home from school.

close

Little Dinosaur is standing close to Baby Dinosaur.

clothes

Here are some clothes. Dippi is wearing a scarf because he is cold.

coat

You wear a coat when it is cold.

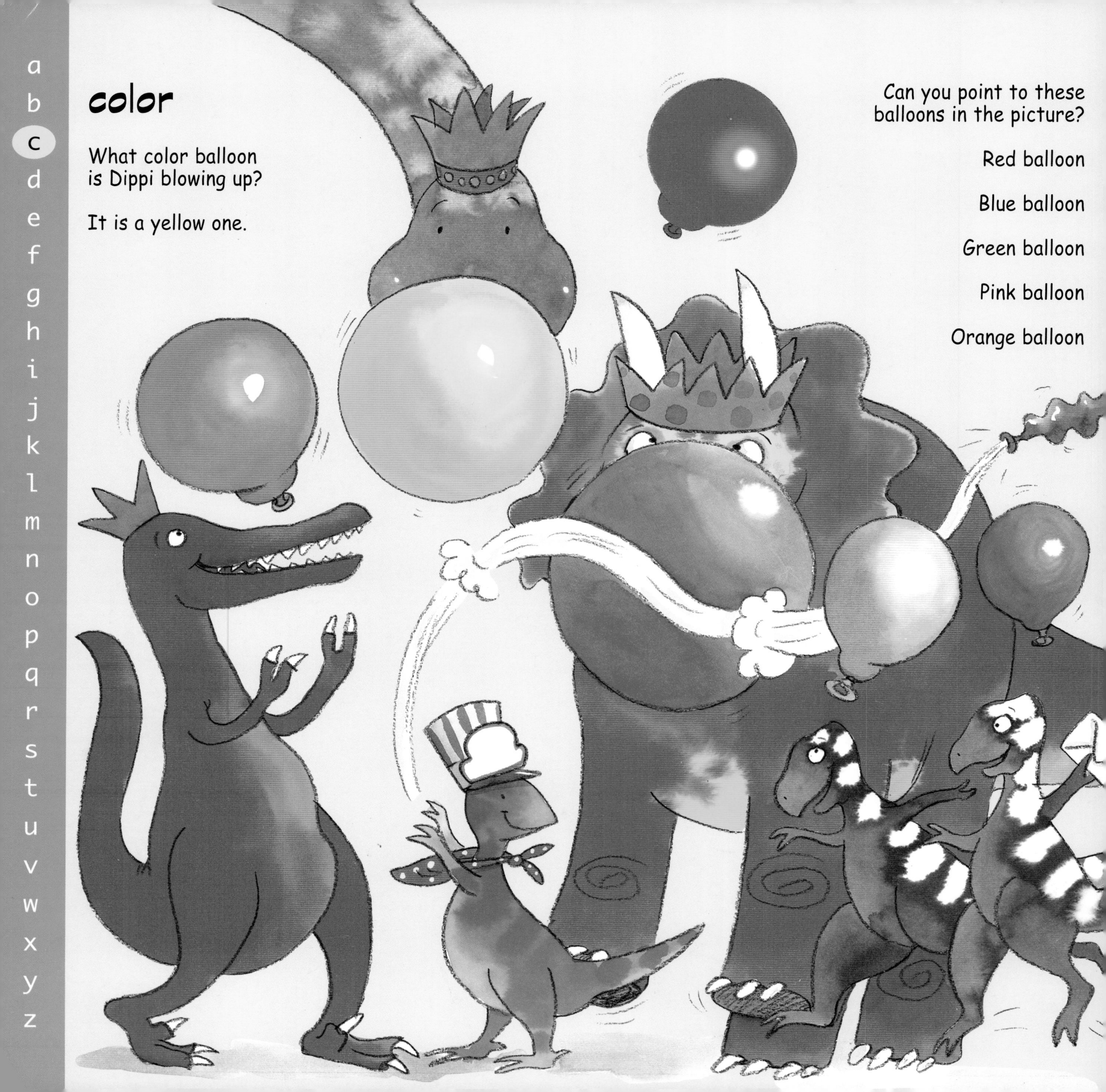

a b c d e f g h i j k l m n o p q r s t u v w x y z

color

What color balloon
is Dippi blowing up?

It is a yellow one.

Can you point to these
balloons in the picture?

Red balloon

Blue balloon

Green balloon

Pink balloon

Orange balloon

computer
Red is playing a game on the computer.

cook
Put the pizza in the oven to cook, then eat it while it is hot.

count
There are six dinosaurs in this picture. Can you count them?

cow
Here is a cow with her baby calf.

crab
Tricky has spotted a brown crab in the water.

crayon
Can you point to the orange crayon?

cry
Baby Dinosaur is tired and hungry. She has started to cry.

cup
Red is carrying a tray with a cup and a piece of cake.

cut
You can use scissors to cut through paper.

Dd

dance

When Little Dinosaur hears music he always starts to dance.

dark

It is dark outside. Time for the Dino Pals to go to bed!

day

There are seven days in a week. Do you know what day it is today?

dig

Little Dinosaur likes to dig with his shovel.

dinner

Red is having spaghetti for dinner this evening.

dinosaur

Tricky is a big dinosaur. Little Dinosaur is a small dinosaur.

dirty

Little Dinosaur is dirty. He needs a bath!

dog

The dog is eating his dinner from his blue bowl.

doll

Point to the doll with the green skirt.

door

Little Dinosaur is going into the house through the front door. Red is following him.

down

Little Dinosaur is going down the slide at the fair.

drawing

Here is a drawing of the Dino Pals' cat.

dream

Little Dinosaur is asleep. He is having a dream about ice cream!

drink

The dinosaurs are having a drink of orange juice.

drop

It is easy for Dippi to drop the ball through the net!

dry

Little Dinosaur is playing in the rain, but Red is keeping dry under the tree.

duck

Here is the duck family. There are six baby ducklings.

a b c d e f g h i j k l m n o p q r s t u v w x y z

ear

You have got two ears. Point to the two ears on this boy's head.

eat

This hungry dinosaur is about to eat his lunch.

egg

What is hatching out of this egg? It is a dinosaur!

elbow

You bend your arm at the elbow. Touch one of your elbows.

elephant

An elephant is a very large animal with big ears.

empty

This glass is empty. It has nothing in it.

entrance

The entrance to the toy shop is at the front. The exit is at the back.

eye

Tricky has two big eyes.

Ff

face

The girl has a big smile on her face. She is feeling happy.

fair

The Dino Pals are having lots of fun at the fair.

fall

Red is standing on the roof! He must be careful not to fall off.

family

Here is the dinosaur family all together at home.

farm

All these animals live on the farm.

fast

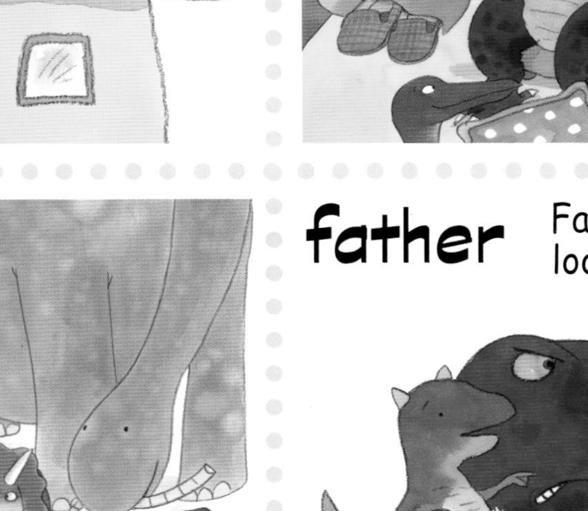

Red and Tricky were running fast, so they are very tired.

father

Father Dinosaur is looking after Baby Dinosaur today.

find

Little Dinosaur is trying to find his friends. They are hiding!

finger

You have two hands, with five fingers on each hand.

fish

How many fish can you count?

flag

Dippi is holding a purple flag.

floor

Little Dinosaur is sitting on the floor.

flower

The dinosaur is holding a flower. The flower has white petals.

food

Some of the dinosaurs are making a mess with their food!

foot

This girl is standing on one foot. Can you balance on one foot?

friend

The dinosaurs are friends. They like to play together.

fruit

What kind of fruit do you like best?

Gg

game

The dinosaurs are on the bus. They are playing a game.

gift

Dippi has a gift for Little Dinosaur because it is his birthday.

giraffe

A giraffe is an animal with a very long neck.

girl

The girl is having a picnic. She has some fruit and sandwiches to eat.

give

Red and Tricky have gifts to give to Little Dinosaur.

glove

We wear gloves to keep our hands warm when it is cold. Here is one glove. Can you spot the other glove on this page?

good

Red is a good dinosaur. He brushes his teeth every morning and evening.

grow

These little lambs will grow into a sheep like their mother.

a b c d e f g h i j k l m n o p q r s t u v w x y z

Hh

half

The cake has been cut in half. How many pieces are there?

hand

Red is holding a paintbrush in one hand and a pot of paint in the other.

happy

Little Dinosaur is very happy. It is his birthday and he has a new yellow ball.

hat

Dippi is wearing a party hat on his head.

head

This dinosaur is wearing a helmet on his head.

hear

Little Dinosaur is shouting. He wants everyone to hear him.

heavy

The picnic basket is very heavy! It is full of food.

helicopter

The helicopter makes a loud noise when it flies overhead.

help

Red wants to help tidy up. He is putting the balls back in the box.

high

The kite is stuck high up in the tree.

hold

The dinosaurs are playing on the seesaw. Hold on tight!

horn

Tricky has three horns on his head.

horse

This horse is brown.

hot

It is hot today. Little Dinosaur is enjoying the sun.

hour

The clock has twelve hours marked on it.

house

The house has a red roof and two blue doors.

hungry

These dinosaurs are very hungry!

a
b
c
d
e
f
g
h
i
j
k
l
m
n
o
p
q
r
s
t
u
v
w
x
y
z
Ii
ice
Look at the penguin. He is standing on a block of ice.
ice cream
Red is eating ice cream.
ill
The little girl is giving flowers to her grandma, who is ill.
in
Dippi is wading in the water.
insect
All of these creatures are insects.
inside
Tricky is inside the house. Red is outside.
iron
We iron our clothes to get rid of wrinkles.
island
An island has water all around it.

jacket

Red has a new jacket.

jar

There are two jars of jam in the refrigerator.

jeans

Jeans are blue. They are made out of a material called denim.

jellyfish

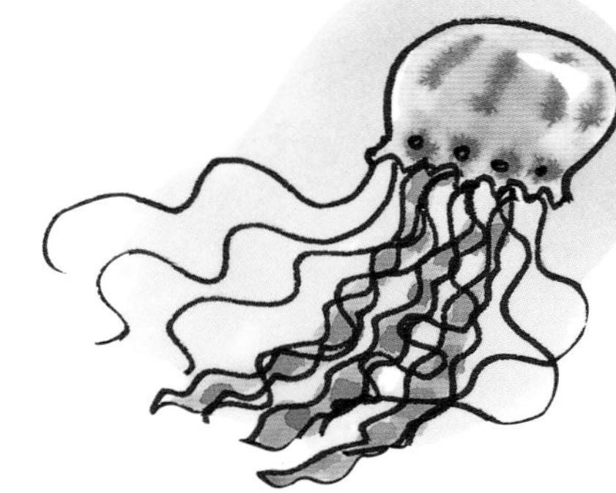

Jellyfish swim in the sea.

jigsaw

Jigsaw puzzles are pictures cut into pieces. You have to put them back together again.

juggler

The juggler is throwing five balls up into the air.

juice

When you squeeze oranges, you get delicious juice to drink.

jump

How high can Little Dinosaur jump? Can he jump over the log?

a b c d e f g h i j k l m n o p q r s t u v w x y z

Kk

kangaroo

A kangaroo is an animal. Kangaroos live in Australia.

keep

Tricky wants to keep his old umbrella. He will not throw it away.

key

Red has a big key. This key will open the door to the Dino Pals' house.

keyboard

Red typed "cat" on the keyboard to find out all about cats.

kick

Red has kicked the ball very hard.

kind

Little Dinosaur is kind. He helps look after Baby Dinosaur.

king

The king has a crown on his head.

kiss

Little Dinosaur is hugging Baby Dinosaur. He gives her a big kiss.

kitchen

The Dino Pals are in the kitchen getting ready to eat.

kite

It is a windy day and Little Dinosaur is flying his kite.

kitten

These kittens will grow up to be cats.

knot

The twin is trying to untie a knot, but it isn't easy!

ladder

This dinosaur is carrying a ladder.

large

Little Dinosaur is trying to put the large blue ball into a large yellow box.

last

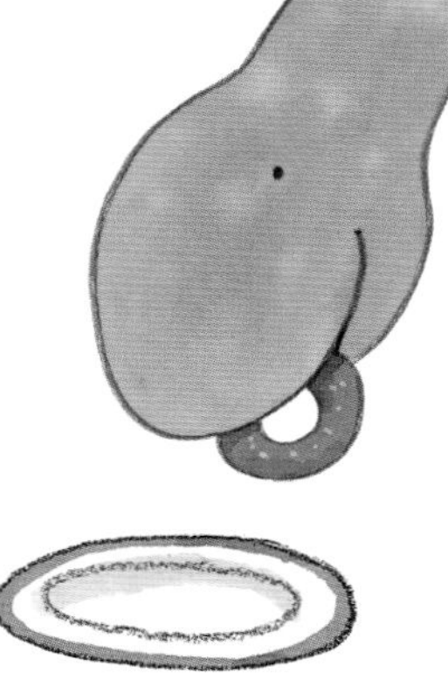

Dippi is eating the last donut. All the others have been eaten.

left

Little Dinosaur has a yellow card in his left hand. The twin has a green card in his right hand.

leg

This dinosaur has two very long legs.

light

Time to turn the light out so Dippi can go to sleep.

little

Little Dinosaur is little. He is a very small dinosaur.

long

This dinosaur has a very long neck.

make

The dinosaurs are going to make a cake.

many

There are too many dinosaurs on the train. It is very crowded.

map

Dippi is looking at the map. He wants to find the way to the river.

measure

Little Dinosaur is going to measure himself and find out how tall he is.

midnight

It is twelve o'clock at night—that is midnight. Little Dinosaur is fast asleep.

milk

These two dinosaurs are enjoying a drink of cold milk.

mirror

Red is brushing his teeth. He can see himself in the mirror.

money

When you go shopping, you need to take some money to pay for the things you buy.

monkey

The monkey is holding a banana.

moon

On a dark night, you can sometimes see the moon in the sky.

mother

These mother dinosaurs are looking after their eggs.

mountain

The Dino Pals want to climb up the mountain to the top.

mouse

One mouse is inside the cage. The other mouse is outside.

mouth

This dinosaur has a mouth full of sharp teeth!

mud

Red has slipped on the mud in the field.

mug

What color is the mug that Red is holding?

music

The dinosaurs have a music class at school today. They are taking their musical instruments with them.

Nn

name
Hello! My name is Little Dinosaur. What is your name?

near
The dinosaur is near the tree.

neck
What a long neck! This dinosaur can reach up to eat the leaves at the top of the tree.

nest
The white duck is sitting on her nest. She is keeping the eggs in the nest warm.

new
Baby Dinosaur has a new boat. It has blue sails.

night
Night is the opposite of day. It is dark at night.

noise
The airplane makes a loud noise when it takes off.

nose
Everybody has a nose on their face. How many noses can you see here?

a
b
c
d
e
f
g
h
i
j
k
l
m
n
o
p
q
r
s
t
u
v
w
x
y
z

number

Do you know your numbers up to ten?
Look at the picture of the picnic and try to spot these things:

1 black bird
2 dinosaurs
3 tomatoes
4 bananas
5 glasses
6 red apples
7 blue plates
8 donuts
9 cupcakes
10 star cookies

Oo

ocean

The Dino Pals are in a boat on the ocean.

old

Tricky's umbrella is very old. There is a hole in it.

on

Tricky is lying on a mat. He is asleep.

open

The bus door is open. But you must take turns to get on board.

orange

This dinosaur is holding an orange. He is going to peel it and eat it.

outside

Little Dinosaur is outside the house. He wants to go in!

over

Little Dinosaur is jumping over the bench.

owl

The owl is a bird. It is flying high in the sky.

a b c d e f g h i j k l m n o p q r s t u v w x y z

page

When you open a book you can see two pages.

paint

Look at all the different colors of paint in the paint box.

pair

These two boots are a pair. They belong together.

paper

The pages in this book are made of paper. So is a newspaper.

party

The Dino Pals are having a party.

pear

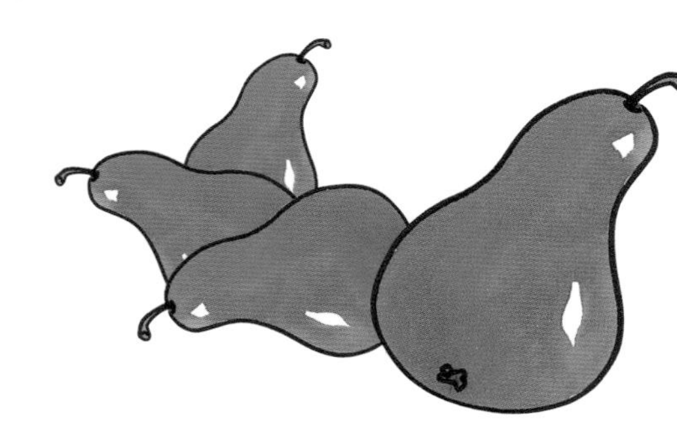

A pear is a fruit. Like apples, pears grow on trees.

pencil

Little Dino uses a pencil to write on the paper.

pet

This is a pet cat. She is wearing a green collar.

piece

Each dinosaur has a piece of cake.

pig

This mother pig has five piglets.

plate

Little Dinosaur has a plate full of cookies to share with his friends.

play

It is time to play! The dinosaurs are playing on the beach.

please

"Please can I have a turn?" Tricky asks politely.

pretty

The girl is wearing a pretty pink dress.

puddle

Little Dinosaur is splashing in the puddle. He is having fun!

pull

push

Tricky is trying to pull the heavy cart. Red is trying to push it.

a b c d e f g h i j k l m n o p q r s t u v w x y z

quarrel

Please don't quarrel Dino Pals!
Share your toys and be friends.

quarter

This cake has been cut into four big pieces. Each piece is one quarter of the cake.

queen

The queen is wearing a blue dress. She has a crown on her head.

question

The Dino Pals have a question to ask. "Will you take us out for the day?"

quiet

Be quiet when you are watching a movie. Don't make a noise.

rabbit

Mother rabbit is asleep with her babies. How many baby rabbits can you see?

race

Red and Tricky have had a race. Little Dinosaur was timing them.

rain

It has started to rain.
Tricky is sheltering under a tree.

rainbow

When it is raining and the sun is shining, look for a rainbow in the sky.

read

Tricky likes to read. He has lots of books.

ride

The dinosaurs are out for a ride in the bus. They are going to the park to play.

river

The river runs through the fields near the farm.

road

The children are crossing the road to get to school.

rock

Little Dinosaur is looking underneath the big gray rock.

roof

The house has a red roof and a green front door.

run

This dinosaur can run very fast. Nobody can catch him.

Ss

sad

Tricky is sad. He has dropped his ice cream.

same

These two dinosaurs look exactly the same. They are twins.

sand

The Dino Pals are on the beach. They love playing in the sand.

sandwich

Red is hungry. He is going to eat a sandwich.

scarecrow

The scarecrow stands in the farmer's cornfield to scare away the birds who eat the corn.

scarf

When it is cold, it is a good idea to wear a scarf around your neck.

school

In school, the dinosaurs learn about the seasons.

see

Can you see Baby Dinosaur in this picture?

shape

What shape is this book? It is square. Here are some other shapes. Look at them, then see if you can find them on or around Little Dinosaur's cake.

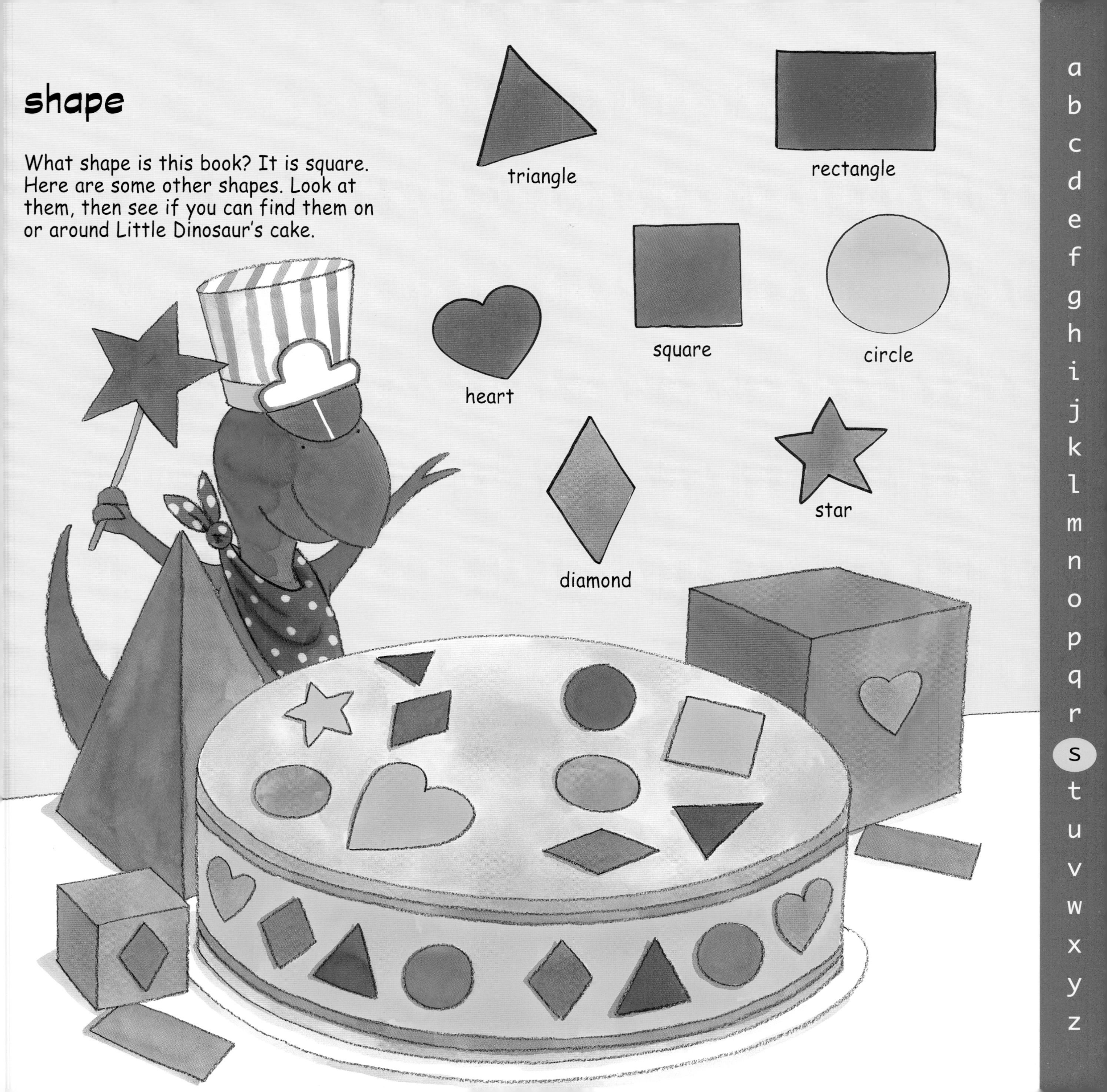

a b c d e f g h i j k l m n o p q r s t u v w x y z

sheep

The sheep has a woolly coat.

ship

A ship is a big boat that sails across the ocean.

shoe

Little Dinosaur is carrying a basket full of shoes. He has dropped one shoe.

shut

The gate is shut. The dinosaur is mad because he cannot open it.

sit

Red likes to sit on a rock and look at the sea.

sleep

At night, Little Dinosaur goes to sleep in his bed.

small

Red is putting the smallest balls in the small box.

snow

In the winter, when there is snow on the ground, the dinosaurs like to build a snowman.

soap

There is a bar of yellow soap on the sink.

sock
Little Dinosaur is looking for a red sock. Can you see it?
spoon
Dippi is holding a spoon. He is putting sugar into the cup of coffee.
spot
Dippi has a yellow blanket with red spots.
star
At night you can see stars in the sky
stripe
This dinosaur has six orange stripes and one purple stripe.
stop
Stop squeezing the toothpaste tube, Tricky!
sun
Red likes to lie in the sun.
sweet
Little Dinosaur is looking at the cakes and ice cream. He loves to eat sweet things.
swim
Red is going for a swim. "Come and join me!" he calls.
a b c d e f g h i j k l m n o p q r s t u v w x y z

Tt

table

This table has got lots of things on it. Can you point to the book on the table?

tail

Little Dinosaur has a green tail.

talk

The twins talk to each other all the time. They never stop talking!

tall

One tree is tall. It reaches up toward the sun. The other tree is short.

teacher

A teacher helps us learn new things.

teeth

This dinosaur brushes his teeth to keep them white.

telephone

Little Dinosaur likes to answer the telephone when it rings.

television

The dinosaurs are watching television before bedtime.

throw

Little Dinosaur is trying to throw the ball high into the air.

time

It is time for the dinosaurs to stop playing and come back to the classroom.

tongue

Red is licking his ice cream with his tongue.

top

One of the twins has climbed to the top of the ladder.

towel

Red has a new towel. He will use it to dry himself when he goes swimming.

toy

Little Dinosaur is playing with his toy train and his toy bear.

tractor

When they visit the farm, the Dino Pals see a red tractor.

train

The Dino Pals are on the train. They are going on a trip to town.

tree

Red is taking a nap under a tree.

a b c d e f g h i j k l m n o p q r s t u v w x y z

umbrella

It is starting to rain and Little Dinosaur has put up his umbrella.

under

Today is sunny, so Little Dinosaur is sitting under a big sunshade to keep cool.

up

This twin is climbing up the ladder. He wants to reach his brother at the top.

upside down

One twin is standing on his head. He is upside down!

upstairs

Red is going upstairs to find his favorite toy.

Vv

valley

Between the hills is a valley with a stream.

vase

The teacher has a vase of flowers on his desk.

vegetable

Here are some different vegetables.
Which are your favorites?

violin

Little Dinosaur is learning to play the violin.

visit

The dinosaurs are going to visit their friends in the next town.

volcano

Don't get too close to the volcano!
Hot steam and rocks are coming out of the top.

a b c d e f g h i j k l m n o p q r s t u v w x y z

Ww

walk

The Dino Pals are going for a walk.

wall

The dinosaur is behind the wall. He is looking over it.

wash

Red and Tricky have muddy feet. They need to wash them.

water

The Dino Pals enjoy playing in the water.

weather

The weather changes. Sometimes the sun shines. Sometimes it is cold. Today there is a storm!

weigh

The twins both weigh exactly the same.

wet

Tricky is running into the water. His feet are wet. Soon he will be wet all over!

whale

A whale is a huge animal that lives in the ocean.

wheel

This bicycle has two wheels.

windmill

When the wind blows, the sails on the windmill turn round and round.

window

Dippi is outside the house. He is looking in through the window.

wing

A bird has wings, so does an airplane.

wizard

The wizard is holding his magic wand.

wood

This table is made of wood. The wood comes from a tree.

world

Our world is planet Earth.

write

Little Dinosaur is learning to write the alphabet.

a b c d e f g h i j k l m n o p q r s t u v w x y z

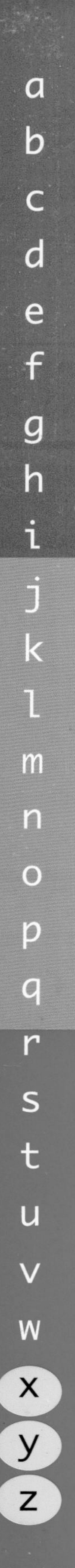

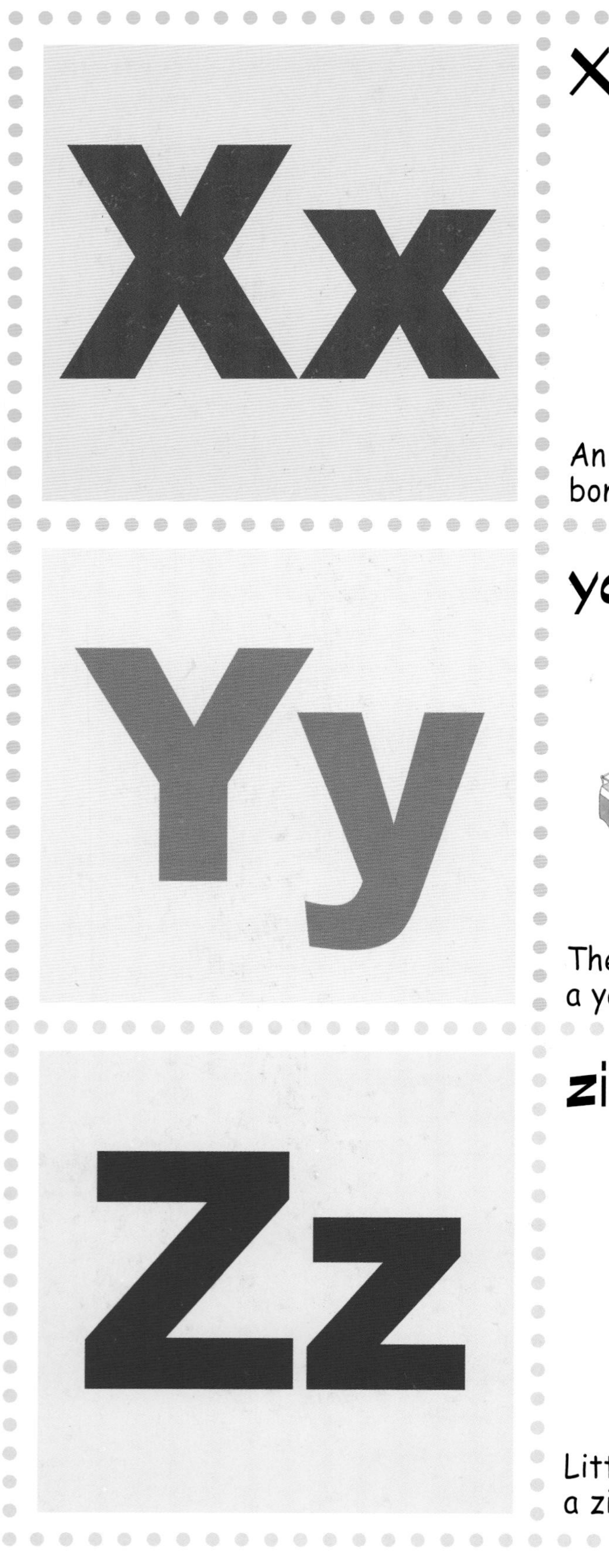

X-ray

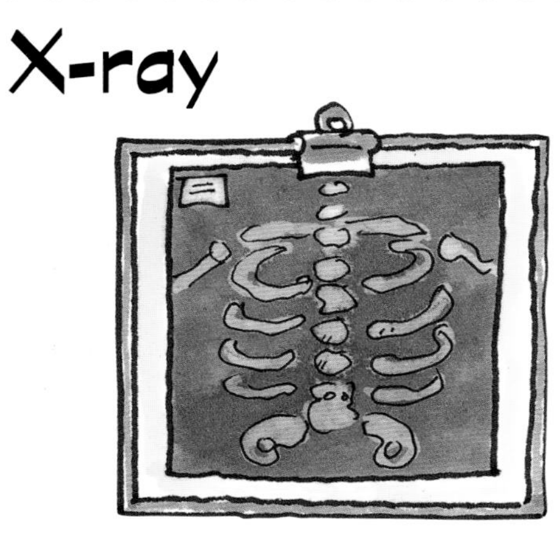

An X-ray is a picture of the bones inside your body.

xylophone

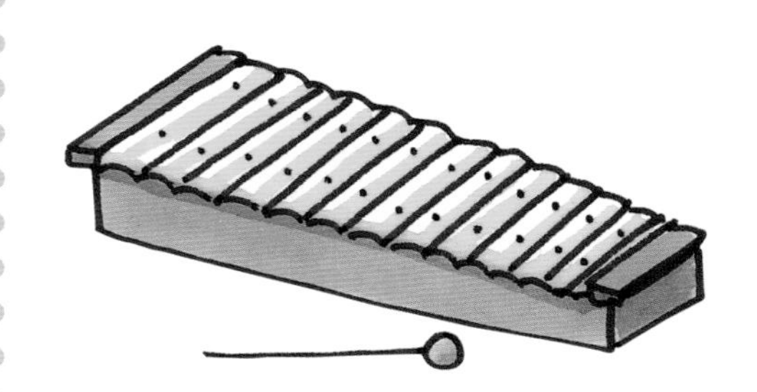

A xylophone is a musical instrument. You hit the keys with a mallet.

yacht

The Dino Pals are sailing on a yacht. It has blue sails.

yo-yo

The yellow dinosaur has two yo-yos, one in each hand.

zigzag

Little Dinosaur's bathrobe has a zigzag pattern on it.

zebra

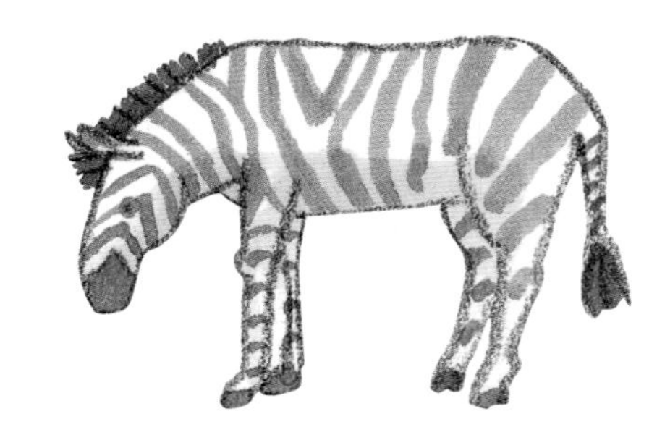

A zebra looks like a horse with black and white stripes.